Hack Your Mind

*Unleash the Hidden Power of Your
Subconscious Mind, Learn How to Bend
Reality and Become Limitless*

Nicholas Hill

nicholashillbooks@gmail.com

Contents

Introduction

Are you aware that your mind is tremendously powerful? That it can shape your reality? That you can consciously tap the power of your mind to heal even your body? Find out from Mr. Wright's story.

Mr. Wright was diagnosed with lymphosarcoma, an advanced cancer in 1957, and was treated by Dr. West. All efforts had proved abortive and time was running out. Tumors filled Mr. Wright's chest, neck, armpits, and groin; each tumor was almost the size of an orange. His chest was filled with milky fluid so much that it had to be drained so he could breathe. With these and many more symptoms, Dr. West didn't expect that Mr. Wright would last for a week.

Mr. Wright, on the other hand, desired to live; he didn't want to die. He put his trust in a new drug called Krebiozen. He pleaded with Dr. West to administer this drug to him. However, Mr. Wright didn't qualify to receive the medication because it was only administered to people who were believed to have about three months or more left before they die.

Mr. Wright refused to give up; he believed in his mind that if he were treated with that drug, he would be whole. When Dr. West discovered that Mr. Wright was bent on having this new drug administered on him, he reluctantly injected him with the new drug on a Friday.

To his pleasant surprise, the following Monday, Dr. West saw Mr. Wright walking around; he had left the bed. His orange-sized tumors had melted to half the original size. Ten days after the initial dose of Krebiozen was administered to Mr. Wright, he left the hospital cancer free.

Mr. Wright was hale and hearty for about two months until he began reading that Scientists have discovered that Krebiozen was not effective. He believed what he read from the literature and became depressed, and he went down with cancer again. He was taken back to the hospital, and this time, Dr. West wanted to help him. He lied to him that it was some of the initial supplies of the drug that deteriorated and became less effective; he said he had pure concentrated Krebiozen which he could administer to Mr. Wright.

Dr. West only injected Mr. Wright with distilled water, and he became well again. The tumors melted, the fluids dried up and he was up and running for another two months.

After two months, the American Medical Association announced that a nationwide study of Krebiozen had been carried out and that the study concluded that the drug was worthless. Mr. Wright believed this and lost faith in his treatment. He went down with cancer again and died within two days.

Mr. Wright's story is a classic of the demonstration of the power of the mind. If he knew about hacking the mind – the powerful information that you will be exposed to as you read this book, he would have lived longer. Apparently, it was not the medication that healed him; rather, it was his mind.

There are two parts of the human mind - the conscious and the subconscious. While the conscious mind is responsible for logic and reasoning, the subconscious mind is responsible for the involuntary actions.

The conscious mind feeds the subconscious mind. If you remember when you were learning to do something new, say ride a bicycle. You focused your mind on the tactics of riding, controlling the handle, looking at the road and peddling. At this point, you couldn't think of something else; your mind had to be in what you were doing or else, you would fall.

However, after some time, you noticed that you could ride a bicycle while you were thinking about something else and not fall. What happened was that at the initial stage of learning, you were using your conscious mind, but after doing the riding over and over again, the conscious mind was sending information to the subconscious.

At that point of mastery, it is the subconscious mind controlling your riding, and this is why you can think about something else with your conscious mind.

David Cuschieri says *"the mind is a powerful force. It can enslave us or empower us. It can plunge us into the depths of misery or take us to the heights of ecstasy. Learn to use the power wisely."*

It is evident from this quote that as powerful as the mind is, it can be hacked. You can learn to annex the power of your mind, and that is what this book is all about.

Irrespective of the state you are at the moment, you can change the way you think and reprogram your mind. You are not too old neither are you too young to do this. In this book, you will learn simple, practical, tested and trusted steps to hack into your mind and annex its power to move your life forward. You can achieve your dreams; you can make it in life, if you follow the nuggets in this book, you will be able to create that life that you desire by the power of your mind.

Let's jump right in.

Chapter 1: What is Mind Hacking and How It Helps?

"What we think determines what happens to us, so if we want to change our lives, we need to stretch our minds."

~Wayne Dyer

When most people hear the word 'hacker,' all they think about is someone writing tons of code to either steal money, disrupt the security apparatus set up in a location, or commit some other crime by using technology.

However, the concept of mind-hacking that we are talking about here has to do with annexing the power of your mind to create the kind of life you desire. It has been discovered that your thoughts agglomerate to form your beliefs, your beliefs combine to form your habits, your habits determine your actions and your actions determine the kind of life you will have.

Mind-hacking is the process of looking deep into your mind to control the source of all actions – your thoughts.

I want to share stories of several great people throughout history that hacked their minds to create the kind of life they desire with you. These stories will help you to see the importance of hacking the mind. They will also make you discover that without hacking the mind, we would not be able to do anything worthwhile in this world.

Abraham Lincoln grew up in rural Kentucky. If you already know that he became a President of the United States of America, you will think he grew up with a silver spoon in his mouth, but the opposite is the case. His father was not educated, and his mother who taught him to read and write died while he was only nine. He was thereafter lent out to farmers who needed laborers to work for them. Now, you are wondering, how then did he rise to become the president of the United States? The simple answer is he hacked his mind by reprogramming his thoughts, beliefs, actions and finally he got the desired results.

With great passion, commitment and determination, Lincoln used literature to hack his mind. This helped him meet up with the demands of success. He built his mind with the writings of Shakespeare and Aesop. He developed his mind so much that it is believed that some of the knowledge Lincoln had about 150 years ago is still exceptional today.

Also, after he became the president of the United States, Lincoln appointed the men he defeated to his cabinet. He was a revolutionary leader that many leaders look up to today. All these feats were achieved because he hacked his mind and used it to create the kind of life he desired.

Before founding the Foot Locker Company, Frank Woolworth worked at a dry goods store. At that time, his boss did not allow him to wait on customers because he didn't have the required skills. Woolworth hacked into his mind and was able to change his life so much that when he started the Foot Locker Company, it became one of the biggest marketing chains in the world.

Kristen Haded started a company named Student Maid shortly after she graduated from college at 21. While she was at college, she desired a pair of jeans but didn't have enough resources to purchase it. She put an ad on craigslist that she was available if anyone needed someone to clean the house. Fortunately for her, someone answered the ad. This person taught her how to clean a house and also hired her every week.

When she completed her studies at college, she got a cleaning contract that she could not complete by herself, so, she hired some students to work with her. Her experience was not good at all. She failed woefully as a leader. About seventy-five percent of the students working with her resigned in one day. It was at this point that she saw the need to hack her mind. She started learning about leadership, changing her thoughts, beliefs, habits, and actions. The result of this hack was that she became an exceptional leader with better, and happy team members. Now, she teaches others how to lead.

From these stories you must have discovered that there is always a clear difference between the life of individuals before and after hacking their minds. Life becomes better, and more impactful when the mind is hacked.

Benefits of a Hacked Mind

Some of the benefits of hacking the mind are discussed below.

- **Hacking your mind helps to live a purposeful life:** Many people are living life by chance, those who hack their minds live by choice. They can make things happen when they want to, they can choose their feelings, emotions, behaviors, among others. Nothing in life overpowers them.

- **Healings:** When the mind is hacked, the individual can experience healing from ailments that have to do with emotions and feelings like depression, panic disorders, among others. Individuals with hacked minds can control their brains to create a new order which will result in healing for their bodies.

- **Creativity:** When the mind is hacked, an individual experience heightened creativity. People who live with hacked minds have better ideas than those who live carelessly. Creativity is heightened with the hacking of the mind.

Chapter 2: How Neuroplasticity is A Boon for Your Mind

"Pushing our self-past our boundaries of limitation and extreme, sometimes to something that knocks off our comfort zone, it creates new neuro-pathways with our brain, we become smarter, wiser, more clarity, our life becomes more fulfilling. Only because we have a totally new experience. We get a new brain with that. Neuroplasticity"

~Angie Karan

Neuroplasticity is also referred to as brain plasticity. It is the ability of the brain to experience change or alteration throughout the life of an individual. Put differently; neuroplasticity is the process through which the brain experiences alteration in the neural synapses and pathways as a result of environmental, and behavioral changes. Neuroplasticity simple means that the activities of the brain associated with a given function of the brain can be moved to a different location in the brain, and this may result in the strength or weakness of an individual.

Neuroplasticity can be seen at different levels. It reflects in little changes in the neurons of individuals as well as significant changes such as cortical remapping in reaction to an injury. To understand neuroplasticity, you can think of the brain as a film placed inside a camera. If you photograph a tree, for example, you expose the film to a piece of new information, and the film responds by adjusting itself to save the information of the tree photographed. If you shoot an animal again, the film's makeup readjusts itself to save the information of the animal. In the same way, the composition of the brain changes when it comes in contact with new information, to the end that it may retain that information.

The process of neuroplasticity is not always straightforward and fast. It can involve many processes and can take place throughout a lifetime. In addition to changing the neural synapses and pathways, neuroplasticity can include alterations to neurons, glial cells (supporting cells for nervous system, as they surround neurons together, supply nutrients and oxygen etc) and vascular cells (for transporting fluid and nutrients internally). It can also co-occur with synaptic pruning. Synaptic pruning is the process by which the brain removes neural connections that are no longer needed while solidifying the important ones. Your experiences and the frequency of neural connections determine which connections your brain will prune out. Summarily, neuroplasticity is a process by which the brain fine-tunes itself for effectiveness.

Neuroplasticity continues to happen as you grow in age and as you expose your brain to new data by learning and memorizing them. Also, it can be incited by physical traumas. When physical traumas spur neuroplasticity, it works as an adaptive mechanism that permits an individual to compensate for the loss of a function after experiencing injury to the body. For example, if an individual is involved in an accident that affects the brain, neuroplasticity permits the brain to "reinvent" or "rewire" itself to reestablish and maximize the functioning of the brain by reconstructing neural circuits and sending signals to the whole brain parts to take over the injured parts.

This amazing story of a girl named Cameron Mott proves the vast potential of neuroplasticity on our body's re-inventing abilities.

Around the age of three years Cameron started having violent seizures. She started suffering badly from it and eventually she started losing her ability to speak. She was diagnosed with a disease called Rasmussen's encephalitis, a rare inflammatory neurological disease. Ironically the only real treatment for this was hemispherectomy—cutting out half of her brain.

It was not a simple surgery as the aftermath of this surgery was supposed to more traumatic for little Cameron, as one half of your brain controls and is responsible for movement and sensation in the other half of your body, i.e., the left hemisphere controls the right side of your entire body's function and similarly the right brain controls the left side. The surgery therefore would mean that Cameron would live entire life suffering from paralysis of one side of the body due to removing half the brain.

Anyways the surgery was conducted and to the surprise of everyone, within four weeks post-operation, she walked out of the hospital. Not only that within few months of rehabilitation, she joined her school with a normal health and doing all the activities normally like other human beings, which was not less than any miracles for the doctors. No more seizure and despite removing half brain she could live a normal life without any kind of paralysis.

This was possible because remaining half portion of Cameron's brain sensed the massive loss of neural tissue and it physically rewired and reorganized itself to take over everything that the other half had previously handled.

Neuroplasticity is more evident in children than adults. This does not mean that it doesn't happen at all in adults, it does. The potential for neuroplasticity to take place in adults generally than it is in children; however, with continued efforts and a healthy routine, adults can induce and encourage positive alterations and development in their brains as the children.

There are two main types of neuroplasticity:

Structural neuroplasticity describes the changes in the brain which only occurs in the strength of the networks between neurons, and

Functional neuroplasticity, which according to describes the constant changes induced in synapses as a result of learning and development.

According to Christopher Bergland, "one could speculate that this process opens up the possibility to reinvent yourself and move away from the status quo or to overcome past traumatic events that evoke anxiety and stress. Hardwired fear-based memories often lead to avoidance behaviors that can hold you back from living your life to the fullest." To support this quote, I will share examples of people who have used neuroplasticity to overcome past traumatic events and move away from the status quo.

Dr. David J. Hellerstein, a research psychiatrist at the New York State Psychiatric Institute, and Professor of Clinical Psychiatry, tells the story of a patient he calls Hannah. Hannah was a 27-year-old single woman who experienced several losses and traumas in her early life. By the time she was presented for treatment, she had experienced over 15 years of critical depression and fright disorder. She also suffered from some stress-induced illnesses which included severe asthma and colitis. Dr. David noted that her depression and anxiety responded to psychotherapy. However, he pointed out that the most exciting part of the healing was when Hannah became passionate about yoga (which is one of the activities that induce neuroplasticity). After a few months of practicing yoga for an average of 2 to 3 hours daily, Hannah was able to sustain a feeling of calmness and wellbeing for the first time in a very long time. Also, the stress-induced illnesses became less severe. This is an example of how neuroplasticity can bring healing.

Debbie Hampton had tried for years to be a perfect wife and mother, but she could not sustain her marriage; she divorced with two sons. Due to the break-up and the gloom that clouded the future, she decided to kill herself by taking an overdose of about 90 pills. After writing a note on her computer which read "I've screwed up this life so bad that there is no place here for me and nothing I can contribute," she took the pills and laid down. Before she died, someone found out and rushed her to the hospital. After waking from a one-week coma, she was diagnosed with encephalopathy (a general term that means the brain is not working right).

Due to this, she couldn't control her bladder, and her hands shook continually. She could not understand what she was seeing. After staying a while in the rehabilitation center, she started to recover slowly. She heard about a new treatment called neurofeedback in which her brain was to be monitored as she played a simple game where she would be controlling movements of characters, thereby, manipulating her brain waves. She discovered that within ten sessions of doing this, her speech improved.

However, her turnaround occurred when her counselor introduced her to a book titled "the brain that changes itself." She discovered from the book that her brain could heal by neuroplasticity. She began to practice meditation, yoga, picturing, and she maintained a positive mental attitude. She recovered fully, and she co-founded a yoga studio.

Now that I have shown you what neuroplasticity is and the benefits that can be derived from using it deliberately, I want to show you activities that can boost neuroplasticity and how you can benefit maximally from neuroplasticity.

Activities That Can Enhance Neuroplasticity

Activities that boost neuroplasticity include:

- Intermittent Fasting
- Using mnemonic devices
- Traveling
- Non-dominant hand exercises
- Learning a musical instrument
- Dancing
- Producing artwork
- Expanding your vocabulary
- Reading fiction
- Sleeping

Tips to Benefit Maximally from Neuroplasticity

- **Start small:** Willpower uses serotonin, and it is required for changing behavior. Like muscles, willpower can be tired and depleted. Therefore, to change your behavior effectively, begin by making little changes one at a time that doesn't need excess willpower. If you make all the changes at once, you will not be able to sustain the new behavior. For example, rather than altering your diet dramatically all at once, reduce one part of the diet. After you have established this change and it has become a part of you, proceed to make the next change.

- **Increase your Serotonin level:** As the serotonin level increase, willpower also increases, and willpower is necessary for changing behavior. So, it is only proper to seek to increase your serotonin level as you seek to alter your behavior. Some of the ways to increase your serotonin level naturally include having a massage, exposing yourself to more early morning sunlight, doing exercise, remembering happy memories, among others.

- **Choose your thoughts:** start to deliberately think about the improvements that you will experience in your life when these behaviors are entirely altered. Use affirmations, positive self-talk, and visualizations to remind and motivate yourself.

- **Celebrate your little victories:** If you keep your focus on the overall goal, you may never reach that goal because you will consistently feel that you are far away from achieving the goal and you will be less motivated. Break your goals into smaller action plans and celebrate your victories as you achieve each of the action plans. For instance, if you want to change your diet, your action plans could include: stop taking ice-creams, chocolates, and doughnuts. If you start with ice-creams, celebrate your victory when you stop taking ice-creams. Reward yourself with something important to you; this will make you more motivated to achieve other action plans that will culminate in the change of behavior that you desire.

- **Choose your friends:** it has been established in research that behaviors and feelings are infectious in relationships. That is, you are likely to pick up the behavior of the people you consistently relate with. This is also in tandem with the proverb that "show me your friends and I will tell you who you are." You have to choose your friends carefully. Make friends with people whose behaviors are consistent with the new behavior you want to form.

Chapter 3: Priming Your Subconscious Mind

"I found that when you start thinking and saying what you really want then your mind automatically shifts and pulls you in that direction. And sometimes it can be that simple, just a little twist in vocabulary that illustrates your attitude and philosophy."

~Jim Rohn

The subconscious mind is like a very fertile soil that bears the fruit planted in it. All the thoughts and conversation you expose yourself to go into your subconscious mind. While the conscious mind can think logically and discard some opinions, the subconscious mind accepts everything it is fed with. Furthermore, the subconscious mind cannot differentiate between imagination and reality. The subconscious mind is what determines who you are; it manages the processes that go on in the body.

You need to hack your subconscious mind because for you to live the life you desire; the subconscious mind must be involved. You hack the mind to reprogram it to be on the frequency you desire. In this section, I will show you how to prepare your subconscious mind for hacking, some things you should know about your brain, steps to hacking your mind, and how to hack your mind's power for enhancing your productivity and focus.

How to Prepare your Subconscious Mind for Hacking

Discussed below are some steps that you can follow to prepare your subconscious mind for hacking.

- **Clarify what you want:** Many people have the problem of not being able to define what they want exactly, and they are surprised when they don't get what they want. To successfully hack your mind, you need to be clear on what you want. What is your desire? What do you want to achieve? Clarity in answering these questions is the first step to preparing your subconscious mind for hacking.

- **Write what you want:** A desire that is not written is at best a wish. To hack your subconscious mind, you have to write in details what you desire. When you do this, you send a signal to your subconscious mind that you are keen on realizing that desire. Write your desires and goals in simple, present tense words that will be easy for a child to understand. Read these desires each morning when you wake and at night before you sleep.

- **Create action plans for your desires:** Action plans are steps that will be taken to realize the goal you have set. Put them down and take a resolve to do one thing out of everything on the list every day. When you create these action plans, your subconscious mind gets a signal that you are about to change your course of life; thus, it gets prepared to go along with you.

- **Visualize your desires:** You also need to use the power of visualization to prepare your mind for hacking. When you see your wishes with the eyes of your mind as if it were already a reality, you are hacking into your mind and creating new codes for it to function differently. Earl Nightingale rightly said, "Visualization is the human being's vehicle to the future – good, bad or indifferent. It's strictly in our control"

Visualization affects the operations of the reticular activating system in your brain. The Reticular Activating System (RAS) is a bundle of nerves at our brainstem that filters out unnecessary information so the important stuff gets through. The RAS is the reason you learn a new word and then start hearing it everywhere. It's why you can tune out a crowd full of talking people, yet immediately snap to attention when someone says your name or something that at least sounds like it.

- **Relax:** One of the ways to prepare your mind for hacking is to take time to breathe, pray or meditate every day. When you relax, your brain accesses newly formed neural pathways, and this is what you need to make the mind perform the new functions you want it to do.

Some Information About Your Brain

As you desire to hack your mind to annex its power so that you can be productive and successful, there are some things you should know about your brain.

- **Every brain is wired uniquely:** I will share several methods with you on how to hack your mind, but it is up to you to work around with these methods and see which one best fits the way your brain is wired. The specifics of hacking the mind is different from person to person. For example, if you are an auditory learner, you will benefit more from using affirmations than visualizing your goals; while a visual learner will benefit more from visualizing the goals than using affirmations. Therefore, as you learn methods from this book, you have to try them out and stick to those that work for you the most.

- **Neuroplasticity:** I have discussed this exhaustively in the previous chapter. Your brain can rewire itself. Therefore, never think that it is too late to learn something new. It may be more difficult especially if you have been repeating the same patterns for a long time, but it is possible. There is no stage you are that it is impossible for you to hack into your mind and create new neural pathways for your brain.

Exercise helps the brain: Even though your goal is not related to exercise, you should also know that doing regular exercise helps the brain to create new pathways. Exercise induces the release of growth chemicals that influence the health of brain cells. It also alters the way the brain protect memory and thinking skills. Therefore, you should consider doing some physical activities regularly. John Ratey Author of *"Spark: The Revolutionary New Science of Exercise and Brain"* states that physical activity sparks biological changes that encourage brain cells to bind to one another. For the brain to learn, these connections must be made; they reflect the brain's fundamental ability to adapt to challenges. The more neuroscientists discover about this process, the clearer it becomes that exercise provides an unparalleled stimulus, creating an environment in which the brain is ready, willing, and able to learn.

- **Every brain has emotional triggers:** Although the brain is capable of reasoning, it does not make every decision from the rational point of view. Emotions and feelings have a strong influence on the brain and sometimes, can superimpose on logical thoughts. Therefore, as you desire to hack into your mind so that you can use its power effectively, you must pay attention to finding out the emotional triggers of your brain and see a way to use them to your benefit.

How To Hack Your Mind

Discussed below are methods and tips that could help you alter the neural pathways in your brain and create new ones that will make you more productive.

- **Use Memory Palace:**

The human brain does not have adequate capacity to remember items in a list as it would locations. For example, if you go shopping without writing your needs before going, you may find out when you get back home that you forgot to purchase a critical item, the total number of items may not be more than 10. But you will discover that you can remember the location of more than ten different spots in your city.

This happens because much of the mental horsepower of humans is devoted to spatial memory, which enables you to learn the layout of your environment. To hack this part of your brain, you can use memory palace.

This is how it works; choose a place that you know well and can imagine without much ado. It could be the layout of your workplace, the arrangement of your house, among others. Then, imagine yourself walking through this chosen location and associate each item on your list to a point in the place.

For instance, if you aim to remember a long grocery list, you can choose to use the inside of your house to visualize it mentally. You could imagine that you had wine on your table, frozen pizza in your fridge, antiseptics in your toilet, and so on. This may look stressful, but when you get used to it, you will discover how easy and effective it is to make you remember a long list. This method doesn't require years of practice.

In a study conducted in 1968, some college students were told to learn a list of 40 items by connecting each of the elements to a location on the campus. The students were able to memorize an average of 38 out of the 40 things, and by the next day, they were able to remember 34 items from the original list; Isn't that incredible?

In another study, some senior German citizens were required to memorize a list of 40 words by relating each to some landmarks in Berlin. Before using this method, they could only remember an average of 3 words; however, after using this method, they could remember an average of 23 words out of 40. This method is super useful, you need to try it out.

- **Write:**

In this age of smartphones, a good number of people don't want to write anything by hand again. Some applications can write for you, all you need to do is to say what you want to write.

However, if you're going to hack your mind, you need to practice writing by hand. When you write something by hand, you engage some neural activities that you don't get by pressing a keyboard.

An experiment was conducted at Indiana University where some preschool kids who were learning the alphabets were divided into two sets. The first set was shown the letters of the alphabet and told what they were, while the second set was required to write the letters as they were taught. When the kids were put into an MRI machine (spaceship), it was discovered that the brain of the kids in the second set lit up. The activities of their neurons were more enhanced and adult-like. So, if you are learning a new language, try to write rather than type.

- **Use your less-dominant hand to control anger:**

Everyone knows the danger of anger; when individuals are angry, it's almost like they are not in control of themselves, they cannot think straight, and they do things they would later regret.

But you can hack into your mind to prevent you from losing control over yourself when you are angry.

A study carried out in the University of New South Wales reported that people who had anger issues could control their temper tantrums better after they were required to use their non-dominant hand for anything that would not endanger anyone like opening and closing doors, writing hate mails, among others for two weeks.

What's the principle behind this, when angry people are studied under brain scans, it is discovered that the outbursts have less to do about excessive anger as it has to do with reduced self-control.

In other words, the primary reason why they experience such outbursts when they are angry is that they have depleted self-control.

Requiring them to use their non-dominant hand to do their daily tasks compelled them to deal with several little manageable frustrations. This increased ability also made them able to control themselves better when angry. If you have anger issues, you want to try this!

- **Boost your immune system by looking at pictures:**

Everyone generally thinks that falling sick is something that we don't have control over. They believe the only control we have is to pay attention to the health tips handed to us by medical practitioners.

While it is not wrong to obey health tips, there is a way you can hack your brain for improved health. By now, you are aware that the brain controls the immune system of the body, and that certain images can trigger physical responses in the body.

For example, some photos make you long for food, while some make you long for sex. Now, let me show you how pictures can help boost your immune system.

In a study conducted by some scientists from the University of British Columbia, subjects were required to look at pictures of sick people for 10 minutes, and their immune system's response was measured.

It was discovered that after the subjects looked at the images, their white blood cells went into overdrive and produced interleukin-6 (IL-6), which is the protein that the body uses to fight infection and burns. You may think that this was just a general response to stress, but that's not entirely true. When these subjects were exposed to images of people pointing a gun at them, there was a 6 percent increase in the production of IL-6, but when they were exposed to pictures of sick people, the production rose to about 23 percent. So, you can hack your brain to improve your health.

- **Reduce stress by laughing:**

Laughter is amazingly powerful. When you laugh, your blood pressure and stress hormones reduce. The oxygenation of the cells and organs, blood flow and level of the pleasure chemical – endorphins increase.

When you are in a stressful situation, you can hack your mind by laughing. Your body cannot differentiate between authentic actions and those that are not, it will send signals to the brain to release more endorphins, and it will help to relieve stress.

Chapter 4: Use Your Mind To Boost Focus And Productivity

"A wind that blows aimlessly is no good to anyone."

~ Rick Riordan

P roductivity is the essence of hacking the mind. But productivity cannot be achieved when the mind has not been trained to focus on essential tasks. The mind has a tendency to wander around several tasks; when this happens, you will discover that you are doing several things but you are not having the optimum benefits from those activities.

According to a study conducted by Microsoft in 2015, the average human has an eight-second attention span less than that of a goldfish. This figure has reduced significantly over the years because of the fact that the brain is constantly seeking for the next new idea due to digital connectedness. Irrespective of the task you are undertaking, focus is essential for increased productivity.

The good news is that 'focus' can be likened to a muscle in the human body; this means that it can be built. With a combination of tools and mindset, you can create an environment that compels you to be focused.

Tips to Increase Focus and Productivity with your Mind

Discussed below are tips that will help you train your mind to be more focused; thus, increasing your productivity.

- **Do one thing at a time:**

It is common knowledge that time resource is limited. That is, every day, everyone has a maximum of twenty-four hours to work. This fact makes many people to focus on several things at the same time. However, neuroscientists have discovered that multitasking drains the cognitive resources of humans. While you may feel that you are more productive by concentrating on several tasks at the same time, the truth is that you would have been more productive if you focus on one task at a time.

- **Make to-do lists:**

You can help your mind to remain focused by making a list of things to achieve every day. It yields better results if this list is made the night before. Set reasonable goals for each day according to their order of importance. Write these targets in a book and take it along with you everywhere you go. Mark each activity as you achieve them. You can also use some apps on your smartphone.

- **Work in 90-minutes cycles:**

A number of studies have concluded that naturally, humans can work with optimum focus for 90 minutes, after this, the frequency of brain activity will reduce for about 20 minutes. Therefore, to improve focus and productivity, schedule your tasks so that you work on a task for 90 minutes, take a break and continue after another 20 minutes. Also, when you are solving a difficult problem, you should take mental breaks to relax your brain. This practice increases productivity.

- **Make your workspace conducive:**

You will need to study yourself and know what works for you. Some people find that certain colors distract them when they are solving a problem, while other colors enhance their productivity. Generally, make your workspace free from distractions as much as possible. Also, to avoid distractions, you may switch your phone off, or keep it in airplane mode.

Chapter 5: Strengthen Your Willpower To Hack Your Mind

"Strength does not come from physical capacity. It comes from an indomitable will."

~Mahatma Gandhi

I n this section, you will learn how to hack your mind by increasing your willpower for increased productivity. According to Gillian Riley, "willpower isn't something that gets handed out to some and not to others. It is a skill you can develop through understanding and practice."

Before we get into the fine details of improving your willpower, let's know what willpower is, and consider stories of people who used willpower to have resounding success in their fields of endeavor.

Will is the capacity to make informed choices. Every human has free will; even if it is exercised in obeying the instruction of other people, it is still the will at work. Willpower, on the other hand, is the motivation to use the will. An individual with strong willpower can decide in spite of strong opposition, while an individual with weak willpower will surrender easily to the opposition.

According to Dan Millman, "willpower is the key to success. Successful people strive no matter what they feel by applying their will to overcome apathy, doubt or fear." Willpower is not all about saying 'no' to the things that will not help you to achieve your dreams, it is also saying 'yes' to the work you have to do to achieve your aim.

According to Dr. Kelly McGonigal, willpower is a response that emanates from both the brain and the body. The response called 'willpower' is a reaction to a conflict going on in the mind. The prefrontal cortex is the part of the brain that coordinates decision-making and behavior regulation.

Since the American Psychological Association conducted a survey in 2011, studies on willpower have gained steam. The objective of the study was to determine the factors responsible for the stress level of the American population. Many of the respondents reported that they were aware of the unhealthiness of their lifestyles, but they didn't have enough willpower to initiate changes. But it is good to note that willpower is not genetic, it can be learned and developed. As you keep reading, you will learn how to build your willpower.

Examples of Successful People Who Used Willpower

Walter Mischel, a Stanford professor, conducted a series of experiments in the 1960s. He and his team tested several hundreds of children around the ages of 4 and 5 years. The results of the research revealed that willpower is necessary for success in work, health, and life.

During the experiment, they brought each child into a private room, made them sit and placed a marshmallow on a table in front of them. The researcher then told the child that he would leave the room if the child did not eat the marshmallow before he arrives, he would reward the child with a second marshmallow; after this, the researcher leaves the room for 15 minutes.

Some of the children could not wait till the researcher came back before eating the marshmallow, while a few were able to delay the gratification. As the years went by, the researchers conducted a follow-up study on the children to track their progress in some areas. It was discovered that the children who didn't eat the marshmallow before the researchers came back had higher SAT scores, reduced substance abuse, and better counts in many other life measures.

After 40 years, the researchers followed up on the children again. They discovered that those children who didn't eat the marshmallow at the initial stage of the experiment succeeded by whatever standards the researchers used in measuring their success. These experiments showed that willpower, which in this case was expressed as the ability to delay gratification, is essential for success in life.

A lot of stories can be told about those who used willpower to succeed even after being labeled as failures. The list is endless, from Thomas Edison who experienced several failures in making the light-bulb but refused to give up, to Elvis Presley who became a king of music even though his first recording was nothing to write home about, to Albert

Einstein, Oprah Winfrey, and a host of others. It is evident from the lives of these individuals that willpower is necessary for success in life.

How to Strengthen Your Willpower

As pointed out earlier, willpower can be strengthened as much as it can be depleted. Discussed below are tips to improve your willpower.

- **Self-Awareness:**

A study was conducted in which participants were asked the number of food choices they make in a day. When the responses were aggregated, the participants reported that they make about 14 choices each day. Careful tracking of the decisions of these participants revealed that the average number of food choices made daily is 227.

This study shows that a good amount of people are not aware of the decisions they make, and you can't change a behavior that you are not aware of. The first step to strengthen your willpower is to be mindful of yourself – your emotions, thoughts, beliefs, habits, and triggers. If you can become self-aware, then you can strengthen your will to make any change you desire. According to Aristotle, knowing yourself is the beginning of all wisdom.

• **Meditation:**

The belief that the processes in the brain cannot be altered has been held for a long time. However, over the last decade, Neuroscientists have discovered that the brain changes based on the behaviors you practice.

Put differently, you strengthen the neural connections for behavior when you practice that behavior, and this makes it easier for that behavior to occur. Meditation helps to train the mind or better self-control; it has a remarkable effect on several skills that are associated with self-control like attention, stress management, focus, impulse control, among others.

The good news is that you don't need years of practice of meditation before you can improve your willpower with it, and you don't have to do it for hours daily. If you practice meditation for 5 to 10 minutes every day, you will discover an incredible increase in your willpower.

Kelly McGonigal, psychologist and researcher explains the benefits of meditation. She says that when we make ourselves sit and instruct our brain to meditate, not only it gets better at meditating, but it develops a wide range of self-control skills, including attention, focus, stress management, impulse control, and self-awareness. Science tells that people who meditate regularly for longer periods have more gray matter in the prefrontal cortex, as well as other regions of the brain that support self-awareness.

- **Exercise:**

Megan Oaten and Ken Cheng conducted a study to test the effectiveness of a new treatment for self-control enhancement. The participants' age range was from eighteen to fifty years, and both men and women were examined. The therapy was physical exercise. Did you just hiss? Wait till you read the results of the treatment.

The participants were registered for free at a gym and were motivated to use it. They were not told to make any other changes in their lives, only to use the gym. At the end of two months, the participants experienced reduced junk food consumption, procrastination, lateness to appointments, television watching; and they experienced increased study, frugal spending, healthy eating, among others.

Again Kelly McGonigal explains that exercise turns out to be the closest thing to a wonder drug that self-control scientists have discovered. For starters, the willpower benefits of exercise are immediate. Fifteen minutes on a treadmill reduces cravings, as seen when researchers try to tempt dieters with chocolate and smokers with cigarettes. The long-term effects of exercise are even more impressive. It not only relieves ordinary, everyday stress, but it's as powerful an antidepressant as Prozac.

If you want to use exercise to strengthen your willpower, don't do too much at the start, prioritize consistency over intensity. Also, it is advisable that you do more of outdoor exercise because science has proven that outdoor activity enhances self-control than indoor activity.

Chapter 6: Mindfulness-Your Mind's Elixir

---

*"Mindfulness is simply being
aware of what is happening
right now without wishing it
were different; enjoying the
pleasant without holding on
when it changes (which it will);
being with the unpleasant
without fearing it will always be
this way (which it won't)."*

~James Baraz

Mindfulness is a fundamental human ability to be fully aware of the place we are and what we are doing without being overwhelmed by happenings around us. Although mindfulness in innate, it can be developed through proven methods and techniques. Mindfulness helps to reduce stress, gain insight, improve performance and self-awareness by observing one's mind.

Mindfulness is a practice that was significantly promoted in the East by spiritual and religious institutions. However, in the west, people and secular institutions are responsible for its spread. Jon Kabat-Zinn, an Emeritus Professor of Medicine and creator of the Stress Reduction Clinic and Center for Mindfulness in Medicine, Health Care, and Society at the Medical School of the University of Massachusetts, is credited for the arrival of mindfulness in the United States.

While he was a student at MIT, he was introduced to the philosophy of Buddhism. Later, he established the Stress Reduction Clinic where he created a program called "Mindfulness-Based Stress Reduction" (MBSR) using the Buddhist teachings on mindfulness.

Kabat-Zinn, in 2013, defined mindfulness as the "psychological process of bringing one's attention to the internal and external experiences occurring in the present moment, which can be developed through the practice of meditation and other training."

More scientists have since taken an interest in studying the effects of mindfulness on the brain. Of note is a Harvard study that revealed that through mindfulness, the brain created new grey matter in areas that are important for learning and memory, self-awareness, sympathy, and introspection. According to Britta Holzel, first author of the paper and a research fellow at Giessen University in Germany, "it is fascinating to see the brain's plasticity and that, by practicing meditation (which is a mainstay of mindfulness), we can play an active role in changing the brain and can increase our wellbeing and quality of life."

Presented below are some facts that you need to know about mindfulness.

- **Mindfulness is not mysterious or vague:** It is something everyone already does; albeit, to varying degrees and in different ways.

- **Mindfulness is not an added thing:** It is a part of our human nature already. The capacity to be present is already present in every human. You don't have to change who you are to practice mindfulness. However, these innate qualities can be developed by scientifically based simple practices that will help us to make the most out of it.

- **Anyone can do it:** Mindfulness does not require a change of religious belief. It only rests on universal human qualities. Everyone can learn and benefit from it.

- **It is a way to live:** More than just a practice, mindfulness helps us to gain awareness of everything we do, thereby helping us to eliminate stress, and make our lives better.

- **It is evidence-based:** It has been proven by both science and experience that mindfulness has positive benefits for our lives. You don't have to believe this to see its work in your life; you only need to practice it.

Benefits of Mindfulness

There are several benefits of mindfulness has shown by different researches that have been conducted along this line. Some of them are discussed below.

- **Stress Reduction:**

In a study conducted by Farb et al. in 2010, the self-reported measures of depression, anxiety, and psychopathology of participants that were randomly assigned to an eight-week mindfulness-based stress reduction group were related with controls after watching sad films.

The research reported that the subjects who practiced mindfulness-based stress reduction had significantly less depression, anxiety, and somatic distress when compared with the control group. This study concluded that mindfulness makes people aware of their ability to use emotion regulation strategies in a way that enables them to experience emotions selectively.

- **Working memory boost:**

Jha et al. conducted a study in 2010. The subjects had three groups. The first group was a set of military personnel who were introduced to an eight-week mindfulness training; the second group was a set of military personnel that did not participate in the mindfulness training, and the third group is a set of civilians who did not participate in the mindfulness training. All subjects in the military groups were exposed to highly stressful events before deployment.

The research reported that the working memory capacity of individuals in the nonmeditating military group reduced over time; the nonmeditating civilians had a stable working memory; while the meditating military group had an increased working memory over time. Therefore, the study concluded that mindfulness increases working memory of individuals.

- **Concentration:**

Mindfulness is associated with an increased ability to concentrate and avoid distractions. A group of researchers compared a set of mindfulness meditators with a control group that was not meditating. They discovered that the meditators had significantly better performance on all the attention measures considered. The study concluded that mindfulness increases concentration and focus.

Other benefits of mindfulness include more cognitive flexibility, relationship satisfaction, less emotional reactivity, increase immune functionality, among others.

- **Improves Emotional Intelligence:**

Consistently watching your thoughts and emotions during the mindfulness practices curtails your tendency to be reactive upon the arousal of emotions like anger or stress and therefore develops emotional intelligence.

Simple Mindfulness Practices

The following are simple mindfulness practices that can help you enjoy the benefits of mindfulness.

- **Mindful sitting:** Most people already know about this. It is a practice where you sit in a comfortable location and allow your mind to be present. You could focus on your emotion, breath, body sensations, among others.

- **Mindful walking:** Some people don't like sitting while meditating, you can also walk around. You can achieve this by bringing your mind to the movement of your feet, the temperature in the room or field where you are walking, among others.

- **Mindful eating:** You can also practice mindfulness while eating by paying attention to your experience of taste, smell, color, and texture as you eat.

- **Mindful speaking and listening:** To achieve this, you must make sure that your mind is present, and you are paying attention to both the verbal and non-verbal cues of the person you are listening to. If you are the one speaking, you also pay close attention to your verbal and non-verbal cues.

How to Practice Mindfulness

As pointed out earlier, mindfulness is ingrained in the human nature, and it should be a way of life; in other words, it should be something you do every moment of the day. However, to develop this innate ability, you should consider paying attention to the tips discussed below.

- **Create time and space for mindfulness practice:**

You should pick a time of the day when you will not be distracted, and it will be wonderful if you can make this time consistent for all days. Such that when it is that time of the day, your body knows automatically that it is time to practice mindfulness.

Also, you should dedicate a space in your house for mindfulness practice. If you can avoid doing any other thing in this space other than the practice of mindfulness, that will be great. Such that your body is notified each time you come to that space that it is time to meditate.

• Be deliberate about concentrating on the present moment:

When you are practicing mindfulness, you must consciously bring your mind to only think about the present but do not judge anything. Only be aware of what you have in the present – the smell in the room, your body movements, your breath, your emotions, among others. Don't think about the past, because you cannot change it; don't think about the future because it is not here yet, just be in the present.

• Don't be in haste:

When practicing mindfulness, you should not be looking at the time; it will distract your mind. Only leave the meditation room when you think you are done.

• Bring your mind back when it wanders:

You are not the only one that experiences wandering mind while practicing mindfulness meditation, don't judge or condemn yourself. As soon as you realize that your mind is wandering, just bring it back to the present.

Chapter 7: How Intuition Helps You Tap Your Subconscious Mind

---

"Follow your instincts. That's where true wisdom manifests itself."

~Oprah Winfrey

A woman told the story of an incident that occurred when her son was nine months old. He had swallowed a penny he found before she realized it. Being a first-time mom, she was set in disarray. However, older family members told her not to panic as such occurrences happen every once in a while.

She knew deep inside of her that something was not right. Her instincts kept screaming at her to take the child to the hospital although he behaved as if nothing is wrong. Eventually, at midnight, she decided to give in to her intuition, she woke her husband and they took the child to the hospital. On getting to the hospital, they did an X-ray and discovered that the penny was stuck.

The doctor said that if the penny had moved slightly, it would have blocked the child's airways and she could have lost the child. Had she not listened to her instincts, her child would have died. The penny was removed, and the child is okay now.

Intuition is an instant knowledge or awareness that does not emanate from human perception or reasoning. It is a feeling inside of you that motivates you to act quickly. Intuition is innate; everyone has it, but not everyone uses it. It is worthy of note that many great business people like Conrad Hilton and Donald Trump depend on their intuitions to help them make smarter business decisions.

Steve Jobs relied heavily on the power of intuition. When he visited India, he confessed that many of the things he stumbled into by curiosity and intuition became priceless to him later. Jobs believe that intuition is more powerful than intellect; if he were to consider the effect of the two on his work, he would say that his intuition has made a significant impact on him than his intellect.

Jobs summarizes his belief about the intuition in this quote "Your time is limited, so don't waste it living someone else's life. Don't be trapped by dogma – which is living with the results of other people's thinking. Don't let the noise of other's opinions drown out your inner voice. And most important, have the courage to follow your heart and intuition. They somehow already know what you truly want to become. Everything else is secondary."

Albert Einstein also believes that intuition is a priceless gift to humans, but that rational thoughts can suppress it. Einstein followed his intuition to have the ideas that birth the outstanding success he experienced. Several hundred, thousands and millions of people have discovered the power of their intuition. He stated that, "Imagination is more important than knowledge. For knowledge is limited, whereas imagination embraces the entire world, stimulating progress, giving birth to evolution."

Benefits of Following Your Instincts

Some of the advantages of obeying your intuition are expressed below.

- It helps you to identify and solve problems effectively; thus, reducing stress.

- It helps you to become aware of the possible danger; thus, keeping you safer.

- It helps your logical mind in decision making.

- It opens you up to new ideas.

- It helps you to develop confidence in your wisdom.

How To Develop Your Intuition Capacity

Having seen the immense benefits of following your intuition, it is essential that you learn how to increase your ability to know what your intuition is saying to you, follow it and rely on it more. Discussed below are some proven techniques by which you can develop your intuition.

- **Meditate:** meditation helps you to focus on the present and to become more aware of everything going on around you. When you meditate more often, you will become more aware of your intuition.

- **Pay attention to little nudges:** The best time to start listening to your intuition is on small inconsequential matters. When you follow it, and you discover it turns out well, that experience strengthens your ability to depend on your intuition in life-threatening situations.

- **Relax**: If you are looking to solve a problem and you can't seem to find the way, you will not be able to hear your intuition while you sit at your desk trying to figure out the solution. You must learn to relax. Relaxation includes but is not limited to sleeping or lying down. It only means doing something else that doesn't relate to the problem you are trying to solve. For example, Albert Einstein once confessed that he got his best ideas while sailing. Also, Steve Jobs often take long walks when he can't seem to find the solution to a problem. You will hear your intuition when your mind is relaxed.

- **Understand Your dreams:** Our subconscious is often the voice of our highest self, that speaks to us in dreams with symbols.

You can even ask your dreams for answers to specific questions and keep pen and paper by your bed to record what comes. Our dreams show us important clues. Harriet Tubman relied on her dreams to lead 300 slaves to safety. Einstein dreamed many of his theories. By tuning into your dreams and learning to interpret your personal symbols and emotions, you will also become more intuitive.

- **Separate emotion from intuition:** Intuition is not based on feelings as many people think. To be sure that the nudge you feel is coming from your intuition, ask yourself if you are anxious, stressed or worried about something. If you are not, then, the most likely thing is that your intuition is speaking to you.

- **Keep a journal:** Write what you think your intuition says to you, and how the events turned out including the sensations associated with each intuition. When you read this journal, it will help you to discover the pattern through which your intuition speaks to you and also strengthen your resolve always to obey your intuition. That way, you will become a master of your intuition.

- **Create or play intuitive games:** You can also strengthen your intuition by playing games that require you to guess. When your phone rings, guess the caller. Guess everything 'guessable.' The more you use your intuition, the stronger it becomes.

Chapter 8: How To Bend Reality And Become Limitless

"Everything is within your power, and your power is within you."

~Janice Trachtman

The story of a lady which I will call Juliet is one which shows that the mind controls reality. When Juliet was about eight years old, Juliet's mother told her that when she learned she was pregnant with her, she told the father that she didn't want another baby. After hearing these words, Juliet's personality changed. She felt she was not wanted and therefore she became unlovable from then on.

Although her mother was loving and committed to caring for her, she could not get those words off her mind. Juliet married a very caring, truthful and loyal man. However, she could not enjoy her marriage because she judged herself unlovable. She doubted the sincerity of her husband's love until the man became frustrated, and she compelled him to withdraw his love for her. Such that, her belief of being unlovable became her reality.

Juliet's story is not one in a million; many other people have similar stories. One sentence uttered to a person can change their lives forever.

According to Dr. Alia Crum, the director of the mind and body Lab, "our minds aren't passive observers, simply perceiving reality as it is. Our minds actually change reality." From her studies, she discovered that people who believe that doing physical work for a living equates to doing exercise live longer irrespective of the amount of exercise they eventually do.

Also, people's blood pressure rose when they were told that a drink they were consuming contained caffeine; of which, the juice did not contain caffeine. That information had the same effect on their blood pressure like when they consumed a drink that actually had caffeine.

Few of the several studies that reveal that with the power of the mind, anything is possible are discussed below.

Alan Richardson, a psychologist, conducted an experiment to prove the power of visualization. He gathered some basketball players and divided them into three groups. This study aimed at determining the effect of visualization on the number of free throws the players would convert. The first group was required to practice free throws for 20 minutes every day; the second group were restricted from participating in practice, they were only to visualize themselves making free throws. While the third group was neither allowed to practice nor visualize.

The results of the research revealed that the group that practiced and the group that visualized had almost the same number of converted free throws, while the converted free throws of the third group were significantly lower. This research reveals that by visualizing, one can create reality.

Dr. David Spiegel of Stanford University conducted a study in 1989 to show that positivity and meditation prolong life. He had 86 women with breast cancer as subjects. He split them into two groups, the first group only received the prescribed medical care, while the second group had weekly sessions of mind support in addition to the medical care. Patients were required to share their feelings and socialize with other patients during the weekly mind support sessions. The results of the study revealed that women who received support survived twice as much as those who only received medical care.

These and many more studies like the experiments of Dr. William A. Tiller, the double silt experiment, the intention experiments, among others, have revealed the power of the mind over reality.

Walter Isaacson, in the biography, *Steve Jobs* states about Jobs: "Throughout his life he would seek to follow basic precepts of Eastern religions, such as the emphasis on experiential prajna, wisdom or cognitive understanding that is intuitively experienced through concentration of the mind."

I surmise that you don't only want to know that the mind affects reality, you are also asking how then can I use my mind to achieve my desired reality? Keep reading.

HOW TO BEND REALITY AND BECOME LIMITLESS BY THE POWER OF THE MIND

By following these simple tips discussed, you will tap into the power of your mind to create your reality.

- **Meditate often:** Meditation energizes your creativity and helps you to have the right motivation to fulfill your desires. It allows you to tap into the power of your subconscious mind by bridging the gap between your conscious and subconscious minds. Design your daily schedule in such a way that it accommodates a moment of meditation. It doesn't have to be for hours, it could be as low as 5 to 10 minutes daily, but you have to be consistent. It will yield better results if you have a space devoted to meditation alone.

- **Visualize:** After you have decided what you want to be, visualize yourself in that position. Just see yourself doing the things you desire to do and being in the places you want to be. You will be surprised how tremendously this can shape your reality.

- **Believe in yourself:** Your mind doesn't know the difference between your thoughts and reality; therefore, you must believe that what you want to achieve is possible. Without this belief, your mind will only work against you. To help yourself to believe, you can use affirmations to keep reminding yourself of the possibility of your goals till it gets into your subconscious mind.

- **Use your intuition:** When you have done some of the things discussed above, at different points, your subconscious mind will send signals to your conscious mind, you have to act on those pieces of information, and you will find yourself achieving your goals.

Some of the other tips that could help you to tap into the power of your subconscious mind include: removing time limits from your goals, positive thinking, and self-talk, cutting down on absorbing unnecessary information that contradicts what you want to achieve, having adequate sleep and relaxation, among others.

Let's Get Started

*"Infuse your life with action.
Don't wait for it to happen.
Make it happen. Make your own
future. Make your own hope.
Make your own love. And
whatever your beliefs, honor
your creator, not by passively
waiting for grace to come down
from upon high, but by doing
what you can to make grace
happen... yourself, right now,
right down here on Earth."*

~Bradley Whitford

I n this book, you have learned the practical steps to hacking your mind; I hope that you have increased knowledge by reading through this book. We talked about the power of the sub-conscious mind, how you can gain from the science backed concept of neuroplasticity and the ways to hack your subconscious mind, You learned about many practices like developing mindfulness habit, strengthening your willpower and building your intuition that could help you to annex the power of your mind. The relevant stories stated in this book have already proven that anyone can hack the limitless potential of their mind, if they are willing and committed.

At the end of this book, it is a harsh truth that nothing will change until you do something. All the knowledge in this book will not benefit your life if you don't act them out. We talked extensively about mindfulness, you will never benefit from mindfulness, except, of course, winning a debate, if you don't practice it. We covered a detailed section of building willpower, but if you simply keep this book aside and don't put the learning into any practice, nothing will change ever in your life.

Therefore the last piece of advice here is to begin to practice what you have learned from this book. Remember, it is consistency before intensity; start small and grow over time. Continue to take baby steps practicing the techniques suggested in this book on a daily basis and soon the magic of compound effect will take over and you will also start seeing miraculous things happening in your life.

Nothing moves until you move. There is no waiting of right time to start doing the right things. Because, as they rightly say.

'The best time to plant a tree was twenty years ago. The second best time is today.'

Go ahead and hack your mind!

Adherence to all applicable laws and regulations, including international, federal, state, and local governing professional licensing, business practices, advertising, and all other aspects of doing business in any jurisdiction in the world is the sole responsibility of the purchaser or reader.